CATS
SET II

Russian Blue Cats

Stuart A. Kallen
ABDO & Daughters

visit us at
www.abdopub.com

Published by Abdo & Daughters, 4940 Viking Drive, Suite 622, Edina, Minnesota 55435.
Copyright © 1998 by Abdo Consulting Group, Inc., Pentagon Tower, P.O. Box 36036, Minneapolis, Minnesota 55435 USA. International copyrights reserved in all countries. No part of this book may be reproduced in any form without written permission from the publisher.

Printed in the United States.

Photo credits: Peter Arnold, Inc., Animals Animals, TICA

Edited by Lori Kinstad Pupeza

Library of Congress Cataloging-in-Publication Data

Kallen, Stuart A., 1955-
    Russian Blue cats / Stuart A. Kallen.
    p. cm. -- (Cats set II)
    Includes index.
    Summary: Briefly describes the physical characteristics of the breed of cats known for their distinctive blue-gray coloring and discusses the care of these cats and what to look for when choosing one as a pet.
    ISBN 1-56239-583-1
    1. Russian Blue cat --Juvenile literature. [1. Russian Blue cat. 2. Cats.] I. Title. II. Series: Kallen, Stuart A., 1955- Cats set II.
    SF449.R86K34 1998
    636.8'26--dc20

                                         95-48186
                                       CIP
                                       AC

Contents

Lions, Tigers, and Cats 4

Russian Blues 6

Qualities............................... 8

Coat and Color 10

Size 12

Care 14

Feeding 16

Kittens 18

Buying a Kitten 20

Glossary 22

Internet Sites............................ 23

Index 24

Lions, Tigers, and Cats

Few animals are as beautiful and graceful as cats. And all cats are related. From the wild lions of Africa to common house cats, all belong to the family *Felidae*. Wild cats are found almost everywhere. They include cheetahs, jaguars, lynx, ocelots, and **domestic** cats.

Cats were first domesticated around 5,000 years ago in the Middle East. Although tamed by humans, house cats still think and act like their bigger cousins.

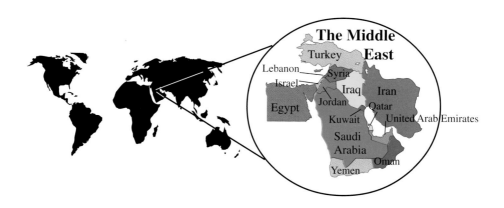

4

The black panther is related to the common domestic cat.

Russian Blues

Russian blue cats have been known by many names. Sailors brought the cat to Europe from the Russian seaport of Archangel as early as the 1600s. Those cats were called Archangels. Other people from other places called the cat the Spanish blue, Maltese blue, or British blue. What these cats had in common was their beautiful blue-gray fur.

The Russian blue is thought to be one of the oldest **breeds**. Their ancestors sailed the oceans and traveled the world. They were first **registered** as a breed in the United States in 1900.

Opposite page: The Russian blue is one of the oldest breeds of cat.

Qualities

Russian blues are quiet, gentle cats. They rarely make any noise. An owner of a Russian blue sometimes will forget there is a cat in the house. Russian blues are very loving to their owners but fearful of strangers. They can be moody and may bite if handled roughly.

Russian blues are strong and hardy. They are healthy, alert, and physically fit. They love to perch somewhere and watch what is going on around them. Blues get along well with dogs and children. They are easy to train and make loyal, loving pets.

Opposite page: Russian blues are very quiet.

Coat and Color

Russian blues have short, fine, double plush coats. They feel soft and silky. People say the Russian blue's fur is as soft as a beaver's or seal's coat.

The fur of a Russian blue should be a solid, medium shade of blue with a silver sheen. The nose and paw pads should also be blue. The eyes of a Russian blue should be emerald green.

Some **breeds**, like the American shorthair breed, are brown, white, black, tan, or grey, with many different markings. But there are only bluish-silver colored Russian blue cats.

A Russian blue comes in only one color: bluish-silver.

Size

    The Russian blue is a medium-sized cat weighing between 5 and 10 pounds (2 to 4.5 kg). Blues have a long, graceful body. They are fine-boned and **lithe**. Their heads are smooth, with a medium-sized wedge shape. They have blunt muzzles and smooth heads. Blues have large ears that are wide at the base, with the tips being more pointed than rounded. They have long, tapering tails.

    Their eyes are round and big. They can see their prey easily with their sharp eyesight. Their strong, muscular bodies are built for hunting.

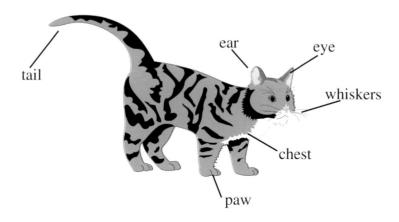

tail, ear, eye, whiskers, chest, paw

Russian blues are built for hunting.

Care

Like any pet, the Russian blue needs a lot of love and attention. A **scratching post** where the cat can sharpen its claws saves furniture from damage. A cat buries their waste and should be trained to use a litter box. The box needs to be cleaned every day. Russian blues love to play. A ball, **catnip**, or a loose string will keep a kitten busy for hours.

Cats should be **neutered** unless you plan to **breed** them. Females can have dozens of kittens a year. Males will spray a very unpleasant odor indoors and out if not fixed.

Russian blues have a thick coat of fur.

Feeding

Cats are meat eaters. They love fresh, lean meat for a snack. Hard bones that do not splinter help keep the cat's teeth and mouth clean. If they live outdoors, they will hunt for birds and rodents.

Russian blues need a balanced diet. For most cats, dry cat food will keep them healthy. Water should always be available.

Although they love milk, it often causes cats to become ill. Check with a **veterinarian** to make sure your cat is eating right.

Opposite page: A Russian blue cat on the prowl.

Kittens

A female cat is **pregnant** for about 65 days. When kittens are born, there may be from three to five babies. The average Russian blue has four kittens. Kittens are blind and helpless for the first several weeks. Russian blue kittens grow quickly.

After about three weeks they will start crawling and playing. At this time they may be given cat food. After about a month, kittens will run, wrestle, and play games. Russian blue kittens are strong and playful with people they know. But they are easily frightened by strangers. Some Russian blues are born with the markings of a Siamese cat. They are called "White Russians."

If the cat is a **pedigree**, it should be **registered** and given papers at this time. At 10 weeks the kittens are old enough to be sold or given away.

Russian blue kittens

Buying a Kitten

The best place to get a Russian blue is from a breeder. Cat shows are also good places to find kittens. Next you must decide if you want a simple pet or a show winner. A basic Russian blue can cost $100. A blue-ribbon winner can cost as much as $1,500. When you buy a Russian blue you should get **pedigree** papers that **register** the animal with the **Cat Fanciers Association**.

When buying a kitten, check it closely for signs of good health. The ears, nose, mouth, and fur should be clean. Its eyes should be bright and clear. The cat should be alert and interested in its surroundings. A healthy kitten will move around with its head held high.

A healthy Russian blue kitten will hold its head high.

Glossary

breed/official breed - a kind of cat, a Russian blue is a breed of cat. An official breed is a breed that is recognized by special cat organizations.

Cat Fanciers Association - a group that sets the standards for the breeds of cats.

catnip - the dried leaves and stems of a plant of the mint family, used as a stuffing for cats' toys because cats are stimulated by and drawn to its strong smell.

domestic/domesticated - tamed or adapted to home life.

Felidae - Latin name given to the cat family.

lithe - flexible, bending easily.

neutered - a male cat that is neutered cannot get a female cat pregnant.

pedigree - a record of an animal's ancestors.

pregnant - a female cat is pregnant when she has kittens inside her.

register - to add a cat to an official record or list of its breed.

scratching post - a post for a cat to scratch on, which is usually made out of wood or covered with carpet, so the cat can wear down its nails.

spayed - a female cat that is spayed cannot have kittens.

veterinarian - an animal doctor.

Internet Sites

All About Cats
http://w3.one.net/~mich/index.html
See pictures of cats around the net, take a cat quiz to win prizes, and there is even a cat advice column. This is a fun and lively site.

Cat Fanciers Website
http://www.fanciers.com/
Information on breeds, shows, genetics, breed rescue, catteries and other topics. This is a very informative site, including clubs and many links.

Cats Homepage
http://www.cisea.it/pages/gatto/meow.htm
Page for all cat lovers. Cat photo gallery, books and more. This site has music and chat rooms, it's a lot of fun.

Cats Cats Cats
http://www.geocities.com/Heartland/Hills/5157/
This is just a fun site with pictures of cats, links, stories, and other cat stuff.

These sites are subject to change. Go to your favorite search engine and type in CATS for more sites.

PASS IT ON

Tell Others Something Special About Your Pet

To educate readers around the country, pass on interesting tips about animals, maybe a fun story about your animal or pet, and little unknown facts about animals. We want to hear from you!

To get posted on ABDO & Daughters website, E-mail us at "animals@abdopub.com"

Index

A

Africa 4
American shorthair
   10
Archangel 6
attention 14

B

birds 16
bone 12, 16
breeder 20
breeds 6
British blue 6

C

cat shows 20
catnip 14
cheetahs 4
claws 14
coat 10, 14

D

domestic cat 4

E

Europe 6
eyes 10, 12, 20

F

Felidae 4
fur 6, 10, 20

H

house cat 4
humans 4
hunt 12, 16

J

jaguars 4

K

kittens 14, 18, 20

L

lions 4
litter box 14
lynx 4

M

Maltese blue 6
meat 16
Middle East 4

N

neutered 14
noise 8
nose 10, 20

O

ocelots 4

P

paw 10
prey 12

R

register 6, 18, 20
rodents 16
Russia 6

S

scratching post 14
Spanish blue 6

T

teeth 16
train 8, 14

V

veterinarian 16

W

water 16
White Russian 18